LAUGH-ALONG
Car Jokebook™

by Stewart Cowley

RUNNING PRESS • PHILADELPHIA

Canadian representatives: General Publishing Co., Ltd.,
30 Lesmill Road, Don Mills, Ontario M3B 2T6.
International representatives: Worldwide Media Services, Inc.,
30 Montgomery Street, Jersey City, New Jersey 07302.

9 8 7 6 5 4 3 2 1
Digit on the right indicates the number of this printing.

ISBN 1-56138-178-0 (package)

Cover design by Toby Schmidt
Cover illustration by Wally Neibart
Interior illustrations by Len Epstein
Station KIDZ RADIO™ logo illustrated by Randy Hamblin
Uncle Bumpy Roads™ illustrations by Fred Shrier
Developed by Joshua Morris Publishing, Inc.
Typography: ITC Garamond

This package may be ordered by mail from the publisher.
Please add $2.50 for postage and handling.
Buy try your bookstore first!
Running Press Book Publishers
125 South Twenty-second Street
Philadelphia, Pennsylvania 19103

Hi, Kids!

Welcome to Giggleland! Here you'll meet Chortle and Chuckle, my Giggle-elf buddies. They can't wait to take you along on some side-splitting adventures. And this is your guide to all the fun — jokes, riddles, and songs!

You'll get to know all about the folks in Giggleland, the Giggle-elves, the Riddler, and even that miserable Morbid, the Gloom-weaver. Your Giggleland guide also includes the words to the songs on the tape. Whenever you play the tape, you can sing right along!

So be sure to visit Giggleland whenever you want to have a good laugh. Remember, a smile turns into a grin, a grin turns into a laugh. And laughter chases the Gloom Mist away! Happy traveling!

Your pal,

Uncle Bumpy Roads

Uncle Bumpy Roads

Contents

The Giggle-elves

Hi! I'm Chuckle, and this is my best friend, Chortle.

We are Giggle-elves from Giggleland, where every day is a happy day.

Giggle-elves have lived in Giggleland since the beginning of time. Although they never grow more than three feet tall, they are quite strong and very skillful at making things. They are always happy, and they love to tell jokes and funny stories. They have very good memories and never have to write anything down.

Giggle-elves like to wear brightly colored clothes. They make the clothes themselves and give them to each other as presents. All Giggle-elves are very kindhearted and try to help others whenever they can.

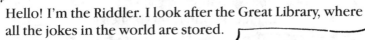

The Riddler

Hello! I'm the Riddler. I look after the Great Library, where all the jokes in the world are stored.

The Riddler lives in an old castle on the far side of the Friendly Forest, near the Marshmallow Mountains. He looks after the Great Library of Giggleland. Every joke that has ever been told is stored there. But some fun-hating people would like to see the Library destroyed, so every visitor has to pass a Riddle Test before he or she can enter the Riddler's castle.

A riddle is a kind of word puzzle in which you have to figure out the answer to a tricky question or problem. A visitor has to answer three of the Riddler's riddles and then ask the Riddler one that *he* cannot answer. Only then will the visitor be allowed inside.

Morbid the Gloom-weaver

I am Morbid the Gloom-weaver. If I had my way, I would banish all laughter and fun from Giggleland.

Morbid is a bad-tempered sorcerer who lives in the damp, dark, dreary, and very depressing Dismal Dell. There he brews the spells to make Gloom Mist. This is the gray fog that makes anyone it touches feel miserable.

Morbid hates jokes and happy songs; the sound of laughter makes him furious. His ambition is to fill Giggleland with Gloom Mist so that everyone will be as gloomy and miserable as he is.

The Glooms of Dismal Dell

I am Grump. I'm only happy when I am miserable.

I am Grizzle. I hate sunshine, flowers, parties, and anything else that makes people cheerful.

KEEP OUT!

THIS MEANS YOU!

Grump and Grizzle are Morbid's helpers. They were once Giggle-elves, like Chortle and Chuckle, but they fell under Morbid's gloomy spell. Now they hate fun and happy laughter as much as their master.

They like rain and cloudy skies, and they can't stand the cheerful sound of singing birds. They want to help Morbid fill Giggleland with cold, gray Gloom Mist to make all the other Giggle-elves as gloomy as they are.

Sing-Along Songs

Everyone in Giggleland loves to sing — even Grump and Grizzle have their own song. Here are the words for all the Giggleland songs. As you listen to the tape, you can sing along.

The Giggleland Song

Let's all go to Giggleland,
Where a merry, laughing band
All wear happy smiles every day.

They've got lots of jokes to tell,
And if you really listen well,
You'll find a smile is never far away.

Let's all go to Giggleland.
We'll go marching hand in hand.
To a place where skies are never gray.

We'll hear riddles, we'll hear rhymes,
Funny stories all the time.
You'll find a smile is never far away.

Old MacGiggle Had a Zoo

Old MacGiggle had a zoo. *Ee-i-ee-i-o.*
And on that zoo he had a lion. *Ee-i-ee-i-o.*
With a ROAR ROAR here and a ROAR ROAR
  there.
Here a ROAR, there a ROAR,
Everywhere a ROAR ROAR.

Old MacGiggle had a zoo. *Ee-i-ee-i-o.*
And on that zoo he had an elephant. *Ee-i-ee-i-o.*
With a TRUMPET here and a TRUMPET there.
Here a TRUMPET, there a TRUMPET,
Everywhere a TRUMPET TRUMPET.
ROAR ROAR here and a ROAR ROAR there.
Here a ROAR, there a ROAR,
Everywhere a ROAR ROAR.

Old MacGiggle had a zoo. *Ee-i-ee-i-o.*
And on that zoo he had a monkey. *Ee-i-ee-i-o.*
With a HOO HOO here and a HOO HOO
  there.
Here a HOO, there a HOO,
Everywhere a HOO HOO.
TRUMPET here and a TRUMPET there.
Here a TRUMPET, there a TRUMPET,

Everywhere a TRUMPET TRUMPET.
ROAR ROAR here and a ROAR ROAR there.
Here a ROAR, there a ROAR,
Everywhere a ROAR ROAR.

Old MacGiggle had a zoo. *Ee-i-ee-i-o.*
And on that zoo he had a snake. *Ee-i-ee-i-o.*
With a HISS HISS here and a HISS HISS there.
Here a HISS, there a HISS,
Everywhere a HISS HISS.
HOO HOO here and a HOO HOO there.
Here a HOO, there a HOO,
Everywhere a HOO HOO.
TRUMPET here and a TRUMPET there.
Here a TRUMPET, there a TRUMPET,
Everywhere a TRUMPET TRUMPET.
ROAR ROAR here and a ROAR ROAR there.
Here a ROAR, there a ROAR,
Everywhere a ROAR ROAR.

Old MacGiggle had a zoo. *Ee-i-ee-i-o.*
And on that zoo he had a parrot. *Ee-i-ee-i-o.*
With a SQUAWK SQUAWK here and a
 SQUAWK SQUAWK there.
Here a SQUAWK, there a SQUAWK,

Everywhere a SQUAWK SQUAWK.
HISS HISS here and a HISS HISS there.
Here a HISS, there a HISS,
Everywhere a HISS HISS.
HOO HOO here and a HOO HOO there.
Here a HOO, there a HOO,
Everywhere a HOO HOO.
TRUMPET here and a TRUMPET there.
Here a TRUMPET, there a TRUMPET,
Everywhere a TRUMPET TRUMPET.
ROAR ROAR here and a ROAR ROAR there.
Here a ROAR, there a ROAR,
Everywhere a ROAR ROAR.

Old MacGiggle had a zoo. *Ee-i-ee-i-o*.
And on that zoo he had a hyena. *Ee-i-ee-i-o*.
With a HEE HEE here and a HEE HEE there.
Here a HEE, there a HEE,
Everywhere a HEE HEE.
SQUAWK SQUAWK here and a SQUAWK
  SQUAWK there.
Here a SQUAWK, there a SQUAWK,
Everywhere a SQUAWK SQUAWK.

HISS HISS here and a HISS HISS there.
Here a HISS, there a HISS,
Everywhere a HISS HISS.
HOO HOO here and a HOO HOO there.
Here a HOO, there a HOO,
Everywhere a HOO HOO.
TRUMPET here and a TRUMPET there.
Here a TRUMPET, there a TRUMPET,
Everywhere a TRUMPET TRUMPET.
ROAR ROAR here and a ROAR ROAR there.
Here a ROAR, there a ROAR,
Everywhere a ROAR ROAR.

Old MacGiggle had a zoo.

Eee-i-eee-i-o!

Grizzle and Grump's Song

I am Grump, and I am Grizzle.
We hate sunshine. We like drizzle.
We like fog to hide the blue skies away.

We hate flowers. We hate trees,
Unless they're old and got no leaves.
We hate rainbows because they're never gray.

We don't laugh and sing.
We hate everything.
Being gloomy is the only way.

Giggleland March — Part One

There was a young man who would giggle
So much that it made his nose wriggle.
When asked why he did it,
He said, "Wade a bidit,
I thig id's dust starded to tiggle."

There was an old man named Keith,
Who sat on his set of false teeth.
Said he, with a start,
"Oh, dear! Bless my heart,
I've bitten myself underneath!"

There was an old man from Peru,
Who dreamed he was eating a shoe.
He woke in the night,
In a terrible fright,
And found it was perfectly true.

A mouse in her room woke Miss Dowd.
She was frightened and screamed very loud.
Then a happy thought hit her —
To scare off the critter
She sat up in bed and meowed.

At bedtime a man from the Amazon
Put the nightgown of his *grammazon*.
The reason was that
He was really too fat
To get his own pair of *pajamazon*.

A fly and a flea in a flue
Were caught so what could they do?
Said the fly, "Let us flee!"
"Let us fly!" said the flea.
So they flew through a flaw in the flue.

There once was a friend of the Sioux
Who into a gun barrel blew
To see if 'twas loaded.
The musket exploded —
As he should have known it would do.

There was a young man from Bengal
Who was asked to a fancy-dress ball.
He said he would risk it
And went as a biscuit,
But a dog ate him up in the hall.

Giggleland March — Part Two

A clumsy young fisherman, Fisher,
Once fished from the edge of a fissure.
A fish, with a grin,
Pulled the fisherman in.
Now they're fishing the fissure for Fisher.

A boy went exploring to Yuma.
And there he encountered a puma.
Much later they found
A stain on the ground,
And the puma in very good *huma*.

A cat told a kitten, "Don't hide!
The dog next door has just died!"
Kitty went through the gate.
Met a terrible fate
'Cuz the cat that had told him had lied.

There once as a greedy young kid,
Who ate fourteen steaks and a squid.
When they asked, "Aren't you faint?"
He replied, "No, I ain't,
But I don't feel as well as I did."

There was an old man from Nantucket,
Whose fortune was stashed in a bucket.
His daughter, called Nan,
Ran away with a man,
And as for the bucket . . . *Nan-tuck-et.*

A young girl from Washington State
Said, "It's cheese with holes that I hate."
Her mother said, "Please,
Just eat up the cheese.
Leave the holes on the side of your plate."

There was a young fellow from Bosham,
Who took out his eyeballs to wash 'em.
His mother said, "Jack,
Oh, please put them back,
In case you fall over and squash 'em."

Giggleland Sports

Giggle-elves love to play games. They love to see how high they can jump using a rubber pole — they call this game wobbly pole vaulting. Banana-skin sprinting, jello juggling and mud skiing are other favorites.

Sometimes the Giggle-elves play elf-checkers. This is like normal checkers, but it's played on a giant board and real elves pretend they are the pieces. Games are usually never finished because the elves get so excited that they start moving out of turn. Soon, even the spectators are running around on the board until they all collapse with laughter.

Life in Giggletown

Giggletown has only one rule: Be happy and help others be happy. But sometimes even Giggle-elves have arguments. And if they cannot come to agreement, Trial by Pillow is used to decide the matter.

Everyone in town comes to watch as the ceremonial Pillows of Law are brought from Giggletown Hall. Each Giggle-elf, then, has to stand on one leg and hit the other Giggle-elf with a Pillow. The one who doesn't fall over is the winner.

Other townfolk often find it very hard to resist joining in the contest. They all grab spare Pillows of Law and, before long, the streets are full of laughter and clouds of feathers. And soon, no one can remember what the argument was about!

Riddler's Favorite Riddles

1. What has eyes but cannot see? A tongue but cannot speak? A "soul" but cannot be saved?

2. What eight-letter word has only one letter in it?

3. A farmer ate eggs for breakfast every morning. But he had no chickens, and he didn't get the eggs from anyone else. How could this be?

4. What clever invention would you need to see through a wall?

5. What does an animal become after it is a week old?

6. When is it okay to sleep with your shoes on?

7. What has four "eyes" but cannot see?

8. Why is a room full of married people always empty?

9. A man was walking in the rain. He had no hat. He had no umbrella. He got soaked to the skin, but his hair never got wet. Why?

10. If a father bull eats three bales of hay, and a baby bull eats one bale of hay, how many bales will a mother bull eat?

11. What bird cannot fly but is always there when you eat or drink?

12. What is the very last thing you take off when you go to bed at night?

13. What's the difference between a hungry man and a greedy man?

14. A dozen people huddled under an ordinary umbrella, but no one got wet. How could this be?

15. Where does Thursday come before Wednesday?

16. When you pick this vegetable, you throw away the outside, cook the inside, eat the outside and throw away the inside. What can it be?

17. What question do you always have to say *yes* to?

18. What question can you never answer *yes* to, even when it's the right answer?

19. What arrives in the cold, goes in the heat, and grows from the top down?

20. On the way to a party, a boy met two men and a woman. One man was giving a girl a piggyback ride, the other was carrying his son, and the woman was pushing a buggy with two babies in it. How many people were going to the party?

21. What disappears every time you stand up?

22. Why do white sheep eat more than black sheep?

23. A dog was tied to a five-foot rope, but it walked fifty feet. How?

24. It's not too hot and it's not too cold. It weighs nothing, but the strongest man in the world can't hold it for ten minutes. What is it?

25. What kind of dog has no tail?

1. A shoe.
2. Envelope.
3. He kept ducks.
4. A window.
5. 8 days old.
6. When you're a horse.
7. The Mississippi.
8. There isn't a single person there.
9. He was bald.
10. There's no such thing as a mother bull.
11. A swallow.
12. Your feet off the floor.
13. One longs to eat and the other eats too long.

ANSWERS

14. It wasn't raining.
15. In a dictionary.
16. Corn on the cob.
17. "How do you pronounce *Y-E-S*?"
18. "Are you asleep?"
19. An icicle.
20. Only the boy. The others were leaving the party.
21. Your lap.
22. Because there are more white sheep than black sheep.
23. The other end of the rope wasn't tied to anything.
24. His breath.
25. A hot dog.

Chortle and Chuckle's Joketime

Chortle: What weird socks! One is striped and the other's got spots.
Chuckle: That's right. And I've got another pair at home just like them.

Chortle: What do you get if you cross a rat with a woodpecker?
Chuckle: A rat-a-tat-tat.

Chortle: Why is the sky so high?
Chuckle: So the birds won't hit their heads.

Chuckle: Which side do you like to sleep on?
Chortle: I don't get to choose. All of me goes to sleep at the same time.

Chuckle: What's the best thing to take into the desert?
Chortle: A thirst-aid kit.

Chuckle: What did the tie say to the hat?
Chortle: You go on ahead, I'll just hang around.

Chortle: What should you do for a sick bird?
Chuckle: Give it tweetment.

Chortle: I used to think that I was a dog, so I went to the doctor.
Chuckle: Are you okay now?
Chortle: I sure am! Just feel my nose.

Chuckle: When I went to the shore on vacation, a crab bit my toe.
Chortle: Really? Which one?
Chuckle: I couldn't say. All crabs look alike to me.

Chuckle: Where does a general keep his armies?
Chortle: Up his sleevies.

Chortle: What's huge and green and sits in the corner?
Chuckle: The Incredible Sulk.

Chortle: What kind of nuts do you like best?
Chuckle: Cashew!
Chortle: Bless you! But what kind of nuts do you like best?

Chuckle: You've got your shoes on the wrong feet!
Chortle: No, I haven't. These are the only feet I've got.

Chuckle: Sure, you can spend the night, but you'll have to make your own bed.
Chortle: That's okay. I'm used to that.
Chuckle: Great! Here's a hammer and saw and some nails. The wood's in the garage.

Chortle: I saw a man walking down the street wearing a cowboy hat and boots. He said his name was Tex.

Chuckle: Was he from Texas?

Chortle: No. He was from Louisiana.

Chuckle: Then why was he called Tex?

Chortle: Because he didn't want to be called Louise.

Chuckle: I saw a cowboy ride into Giggletown. He was wearing a paper hat, a paper shirt, a paper vest, and paper pants. He had a paper gun in a paper holster and was riding a paper horse with a paper saddle.

Chortle: Wow! Where is he now?

Chuckle: In jail — he was arrested for rustling.

Chortle: What's flat at the bottom and pointed at the top with ears?

Chuckle: I don't know.

Chortle: A mountain, of course.

Chuckle: But a mountain doesn't have ears!

Chortle: Haven't you ever heard of *mountaineers?*

Chuckle: I've just finished a painting. What do you think? I'd really like to hear your opinion.

Chortle: Well, I'm afraid it's worthless.

Chuckle: I know, but I'd like to hear it anyway.

Chuckle: What's a crowbar?

Chortle: A place where birds drink.

Chortle: When I took my letter to the post office, they said I had to stick the stamp on myself.

Chuckle: Oh, really? Did you have to buy another one to stick on the envelope?

Chortle: How do you stop an elephant from going through the eye of a needle?

Chuckle: Tie a knot in its tail.

Chuckle: I went for a plane ride the other day and the captain said, "We have just flown from one end of Giggleland to the other in three minutes."

Chortle: Wow! That must have been a record.

Chuckle: No, it wasn't. He was speaking live from the cockpit.

Chortle: What is a goblet?
Chuckle: A small turkey.

Chuckle: I bought a new mirror yesterday.
Chortle: Was it a hand mirror?
Chuckle: No. It was one I could see my face in.

Chortle: I went for a walk in a field with a friend who had never been to the country before. He found a pile of old milk cartons in the grass and got very excited.
Chuckle: Why was that?
Chortle: He thought that he'd found a cow's nest.

Fiction

IT HAD TO HAPPEN by Sue Nora Layter
THE HIKERS by Miss D. Buss
THE SOLITARY MAN by I. Malone
A COIN ON THE SIDEWALK by I. Ben Tover
ROUND THE MOUNTAIN by Sheila B.
  Cummin
THE GROWING CROWD by Maud D. Merrier
RUN FOR YOUR LIVES by General Panic
THE SINKING SHIP by Mandy Lifeboat

CALL ME DUMBO by L. E. Fant
NEVER GIVE UP by Percy Vere
LET'S PLAY PEEK-A-BOO by I. C. Hugh
FALL FROM A WINDOW by Eileen Dowt
DESERT JOURNEY by Rhoda Camul
A BLOW ON THE HEAD by I. C. Stars
TALES OF TERROR by R. U. Scared
THE MAN WHO COULDN'T SLEEP by Eliza
  Wake
ESCAPE TO THE WOODS by Lucinda Forrest
A COLD, COLD PLACE by Anne Tarctic
SLEEPLESS NIGHTS by Constance Noring

Nonfiction

ACHES AND PAINS by Arthur Itis
TEACHING PARROTS TO TALK by L. O. Polly
BE TOP IN SCHOOL by Hedda D. Klasse
MEATS AND CHEESES by Della K. Tessan
FEAR OF THE DARK by Hugo Furst
REPAIRING BRICKWORK by C. Ment
VEGETABLE GROWING by Rosa Beans

ADVANCED VEGETABLE GROWING by
  Artie Choak
HONEY IS GOOD FOR YOU by Ima B. Keeper
ICE HOUSE by S. K. Moe
HUMOR IN UNIFORM by Major Laff
THE POWER OF ADVERTISING by Bill Bordz
THE BEST WAY TO DIET by M.T. Kubbad
A GUIDE TO INSURANCE by Justin Case
EMBARRASSING MOMENTS by Lucy Lastik
GET RICH QUICK by E. Z. Munny
USING EXPLOSIVES by Dinah Myte
HEALTHY FOOD by E. Tittall
SUCCESSFUL KNIFE THROWING by Mr.
  Completely
ENJOYING WEEKENDS by Gladys Fryday

Giggleland Rhymes

I wish I were a little bug
With whiskers round my tummy.
I'd climb into a honey pot
And make my tummy gummy.

A New York lady called Joyce,
Once said in a real Brooklyn voice,
"If you're feeling ill,
I can give you a pill,
Because I'm a qualified *noyce.*"

There once was a writer called 'Wright,'
Who instructed his son to write right.
He said, "Son, write 'Wright' right.
It is not right to write
Wright as 'rite' — try to write 'Wright' quite
right."

If you catch a chinchilla in Chile,
And cut off its beard willy-nilly,
You can put down the blade
And say that you've made
A Chilean chinchilla's chin chilly.

Mary Rose
Sat on a pin.
Mary rose.

There was a young fellow called Max,
Who filled up his pockets with tacks.
That wasn't so clever
Because he could never
Sit down in a chair to relax.

I know a big grizzly bear,
Who has a very nice lair.
It's warm and it's snug,
With a beautiful rug,
And a very comfortable chair.

What's a vampire's favorite soup?
Scream of tomato.

What happens to the claws of eight-foot, 300-pound hairy monsters with three bulging green eyes when it rains?
They get wet.

What does a baby ghost call her mother and father?
Transparents.

Did you hear about the dumb ghost who was out raking leaves?
He fell out of a tree.

Doctor! Doctor! I've got carrots growing out of my ears.
How did that happen?
I don't know. I planted cucumbers!

What happened when the mad scientist swallowed some uranium?
She got atomic ache.

Customer: Waiter! Waiter! This meat is bad.
Waiter: You bad, bad meat! If it's any more trouble sir, just let me know.

When is it bad luck to be *followed* by a black cat?
When you're a mouse.

A mother zombie took her child to the witch doctor. "Excuse me, doctor. Can a child take out its own tonsils?"

"Of course not," said the witch doctor.

"I told you so, Jimmy!" said the mother zombie. "Now put them back at once!"

Did you hear about the crook who fell into a cement mixer?

Now he's a hardened criminal.

Did you hear about the monster that was put together upside-down?

Now his nose runs and his feet smell!

What holds a ghost's bicycle wheel together?
Spooks!

What trees do ghosts like best?
Ceme-trees!

What does a ghost read every day?
His horror-scope!

Young Ghost: Tell me another story about the old haunted house.
Mother Ghost: I can't! It's a one-story house.

How do ghosts keep fit?
By regular exorcise.

Two monsters were out for a walk. One monster wandered into the road and got hit by a truck. "Call me an ambulance!" he moaned, gnashing his teeth.

His friend shrugged and said, "Okay. If it makes you feel better, you're an ambulance!"

A monster heard that the local TV station was looking for acts, so he went to see the producer. "What can you do?" said the producer.

"I do bird impressions," said the monster.

"What kind of bird impressions?" asked the producer.

"I eat worms," answered the monster.

What do witches shout when they are flying? *Broom-broom*.

All the little ghosts in spook school were listening to their teacher. She was teaching a class on elementary haunting. "Does everyone understand how to walk through things now?" she asked.

One little ghost didn't look too certain, so the teacher said, "Well, just look at the chalkboard and I'll go through it one more time."

What's a ghost's favorite desert?
Strawberries and scream.

Two monsters from outer space landed in a small town one night. One walked up to a fire hydrant and said, "Take us to your leader."

The other alien pointed to a gas pump and said, "You're wasting your time talking to that kid. Let's ask his parents."

"I went to a Halloween party the other night," said a monster to his friend. "But I was really insulted."

"Why was that?" asked his friend.

"Because at midnight they asked me to take off my mask."

"So?" said the friend.

"I wasn't wearing one!" snapped the monster.

I've just redecorated my bathroom with some really unusual tiles. They're reptiles!

A man went into the Monster Diner. He sat down and saw a werewolf growling at him from another table. "Is he safe?" he asked the waitress.

"A lot safer than you are," she answered.

Why did the ghost eat a lightbulb?
Because he just wanted a light snack.

Why couldn't the ghost get whiskey at the drugstore?

Because they didn't have a license to serve spirits.

What do you get if a huge giant jumps up and down on Batman and Robin?

Flatman and Ribbon.

Monster: "My family is getting more frightening."

Vampire: "Why do you say that?"

Monster: "When my grandfather was born, they passed out champagne. When my father was born, they passed out soda. When I was born, they just passed out."

Grump and Grizzle's Groaners

Grump: What's that man's name?
Grizzle: It's Ballpoint. He's a writer.
Grump: Is that his real name?
Grizzle: No. It's his pen name.

Grump: I captured a runaway gorilla in my pajamas last night.
Grizzle: That's amazing.
Grump: It certainly is. I don't know how it got into them!

Grizzle: Your hair is very thin.
Grump: So? Who wants fat hair?

Grump: My friend's face dropped a mile when he saw the Grand Canyon.

Grizzle: Did he think it was that disappointing?

Grump: No. He fell over the edge.

Grizzle: What's a frog's favorite drink?

Grump: Croaka Cola.

Grump: Where were potatoes first discovered?

Grizzle: In the ground.

Grizzle: Why did the hen sit on the axe?

Grump: So that she could *hatchet.*

Grump: Why shouldn't you tell a secret in a field?

Grizzle: Because corn has ears and beans talk.

Grizzle: How do you know that owls have short memories?
Grump: Because they keep saying, "Who? Who?"

Grump: What color is a hiccup?
Grizzle: Burple.

Grizzle: Which is the most musical fish?
Grump: A piano tuna.

Grump: How can you cut the sea in half?
Grizzle: With a *sea-saw.*

Grump: What do you call a man with a banana in each ear?
Grizzle: Anything you like — he can't hear you.

Grizzle: Did you like the perfume I gave you?

Grump: Oh, was it from you?

Grizzle: Didn't you see the note with it. It said: "Use this on yourself and think of me."

Grump: There wasn't a note.

Grizzle: Oh, no! I must have put it in Morbid's present instead.

Grump: That's not so bad.

Grizzle: Yes it is. I gave him an axe!

Grizzle: What wears a fur coat and pants?

Grump: A dog.

Grizzle: Sometimes I think I'm a goat.
Grump: How long have you felt like this?
Grizzle: Since I was a kid.

Grizzle: How long will the next bus be?
Grump? I don't know exactly, but at least 25 feet.

Grump: What did Paul Revere say at the end of his ride?
Grizzle: Whooaah!

Grizzle: Will you love me when I'm old and gray, Grump?
Grump: Of course I do, Grizzle.

Grump: Say something soft and sweet to me, Grizzle.
Grizzle: Marshmallows, whipped cream, and angel cake.

Grizzle: Can you stand on your head, Grump?
Grump: No. It's too high.

Grump: Why do you always take a ruler to bed with you?
Grizzle: So I can see how long I sleep.

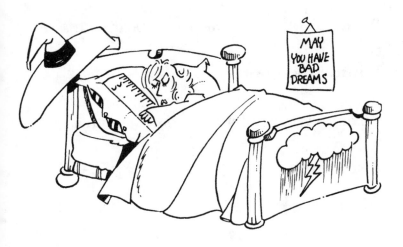

What do you get if you cross a worm with a porcupine?
Barbed wire.

What do you get if you cross a centipede with a parrot?
A walkie-talkie.

What do you get if you cross a bear with a skunk?
Winnie-the-Pooh.

What do you get if you cross a cat with a lemon?
A sourpuss.

What do you get if you cross a rabbit with a firehose?
Hare spray.

What do you get if you cross a computer with an elastic band?
A machine that makes snap decisions.

What do you get if you cross a duck with a match?
A firequacker.

What do you get if you cross a sheep with a porcupine?
An animal that knits its own sweaters.

What do you get if you cross a lion with a parrot?

I don't know. But if he wants some seed, you'd better give it to him.

What do you get if you cross a roadrunner with a centipede?

Who knows? No one's ever been able to catch it.

Giggleland Travel Jokes

Chortle and Chuckle were going on vacation. When they got to the airport, Chortle said, "I wish I'd brought the TV with us."

"Why do you want the TV?" asked Chuckle.

"Because," Chortle answered, "the tickets are on top of it."

When they were on the plane, Chortle asked the flight attendant if the plane went faster than sound.

"No, sir," answered the flight attendant.

"Oh, good," said Chortle, "because Chuckle and I want to talk."

Chortle: Has the Riddler been exploring in Africa?

Chuckle: Not *safaris* I know.

Grizzle: All the planes, trains, and buses are stopping today.

Grump: Why? Is there a strike?

Grizzle: No. They have to stop to let the passengers get on and off.

Morbid walked into a gas station and said, "Would you take a look at my car? I think the engine's flooded."

"Sure," said the mechanic. "Is it outside?"

"No," said Morbid. "It's at the bottom of the river."